The Storm Within

A story of childhood trauma

By: Kamelah Blair

Copyright © 2023 Kamelah Blair

All rights reserved. Printed in the United States of America and Canada. No part of this book may be used or reproduced in any manner whatsoever by means, electronic or mechanical including photocopying recording or by any information storage without written permission from the Author..

ISBN: 978-1-998120-23-9

Published: by COJ BOOKZ

Dedication

"Dedicated to the resilient souls who navigate the storm within, may this book be a guide to healing, a testament to strength, and a beacon of hope for those reclaiming their narratives from the echoes of childhood trauma."

Love KAMILAH

CONTENTS

The Unseen Struggle 9

Isolation in Plain Sight 11

Unseen Pain 13

Looks and Beauty Standards 15

The Weight of Labels 17

Seeking Validation 19

Longing for Connection 21

The Journey to Healing 26

Sensory Waves 27

Therapeutic Tides 34

Empowerment Narratives 36

Steps to Overcome 41

Advice for Healing: 44

The calm after the storm 49

In the heart of the Caribbean, beneath the vibrant sunsets and swaying palms, young Catherine weathered a storm within. Growing up in a humble two-bedroom home, she was the middle child of seven siblings, surrounded by laughter that masked the shadows of a turbulent childhood.

From an early age, Catherine became a canvas for the hurtful words that echoed through the cramped rooms. Taunts of being ugly and too dark-skinned became a haunting melody that accompanied her every step. The ones who should have protected her, her own family, were the architects of the tempest in her mind.

As the years unfolded, Catherine's spirit wilted like a fragile flower in a relentless storm. The echoes of childhood trauma clung to her, wrapping her in a suffocating embrace. The belief that she would never be anything gnawed at her ambitions, leaving them scattered like debris in the aftermath of a hurricane.

Unnoticed by those around her, the signs of her suffering began to surface. Catherine's once radiant smile became a facade, masking the turmoil within. In the mirror, she saw the reflection of the girl they said was ugly and too dark, a distorted image etched into her self-perception.

Yet, her cries for help echoed in silence, drowned out by the cacophony of denial. No one could fathom that beneath the Caribbean sun, a storm brewed within Catherine's soul. The unaddressed wounds of her past manifested in the shadows that clouded her eyes, and the weight of unspoken pain anchored her to a reality colored by despair.

Through the years, the untreated scars of her childhood trauma manifested in unexpected ways. Catherine struggled to form meaningful connections, her heart guarded by the walls she built to shield herself from the torrent of emotional turmoil. Academic pursuits, once promising, became a battleground where the echoes of inadequacy reverberated louder than any classroom applause.

Despite the storm raging within her, those around Catherine remained oblivious to the tempest that shaped her existence. Mental health issues, a silent adversary, were dismissed as mere figments of imagination, an oversight that perpetuated the cycle of her suffering.

In the quaint Caribbean town where Catherine grew up, the echoes of her childhood trauma lingered like a ghostly breeze. Sensory triggers, both known and hidden, weaved their way through her life, each tied to the tumultuous past she sought to escape.

whispers of misunderstanding and judgment surrounded her like a constant breeze. From a young age, she was labeled as the "crazy child," and dismissed by those who failed to fathom the storm of emotions raging within her.

In the Caribbean breeze, Catherine walked the shores of her own solitude, yearning for understanding, for someone to see beyond the facade she wore like armor. The storm within persisted, a silent tempest that raged against the backdrop of sun-soaked skies, casting shadows on the resilience of a little girl who deserved so much more.

The Caribbean nights, once filled with the lullabies of the ocean, became silent witnesses to Catherine's silent struggles. Sleep became an elusive sanctuary, and dreams were tainted by memories she longed to forget. The walls of her two-bedroom home echoed with the laughter of her siblings, oblivious to the tempest that had ensnared their sister.

Social interactions became a minefield for Catherine. Fearful of rejection, she withdrew into the shadows, watching her peers dance through life while she remained a spectator. The whispers of inadequacy that had haunted her childhood became the constant companions of her adolescence, shaping her identity in ways she couldn't escape.

In the mirror, Catherine confronted the reflection of a girl burdened by the expectations of a family that never saw her worth. The once-prominent Caribbean sun seemed to cast a perpetual shadow over her, accentuating the darkness that they had convinced her was a flaw. Yet, her silent screams for validation remained unheard, drowned out by the denial that shrouded her family's perception.

As Catherine entered adolescence, the storm within her intensified. Her once vivacious spirit withered beneath the weight of unspoken pain. In the classroom, she fought battles not against subjects but against the haunting echoes of her family's dismissive words. Academic achievements seemed a distant dream as self-doubt eclipsed every glimmer of potential.

The storm within Catherine manifested in self-destructive patterns. Relationships, when formed, were fragile like glass, shattered by the echoes of unworthiness that reverberated in the recesses of her mind. Each rejection, perceived or real, became a confirmation of the narrative woven by her family—the narrative she was desperately trying to rewrite.

As Catherine entered adulthood, the untreated wounds of her past anchored her to a life that felt like a constant struggle against an invisible adversary. The Caribbean, once a paradise, became the backdrop to a relentless internal storm. The vibrant colors of the landscape paled in comparison to the muted hues of her own existence.

The Unseen Struggle

As a child, Catherine's feelings were met with skepticism and indifference. Her tears, perceived as excessive, were deemed an inconvenience rather than a manifestation of a deeper, unspoken turmoil. The community, unaware of the weight she carried, brushed off her emotional expressions as mere theatrics.

Her parents, haunted by their own pasts, unknowingly cast long shadows over Catherine's innocent world. The pivotal moment occurs when Catherine's third-grade teacher, Mrs. Anderson, notices the subtle changes in her vibrant demeanor. With a keen intuition born from years of teaching, Mrs. Anderson extends a hand of compassion, inviting Catherine into a realm of trust and understanding.

As Catherine tentatively opens up, Mrs. Anderson discovers the depth of her hidden struggles – the sleepless nights, the suppressed tears, and the scars etched into the tender fabric of her childhood. Together, they navigate within the trauma, unravelling the knots that bind Catherine's spirit.

Guided by Mrs. Anderson's unwavering support, Catherine explores therapeutic avenues such as art and storytelling, giving voice to the emotions she's long kept locked away. Through this process, Catherine learns that healing is not a linear journey; it's a mosaic of small victories and setbacks, each contributing to the larger tapestry of recovery.

This worked for her while at school but she hid her work when she got home under a floorboard outside the house.

Mrs Anderson Recognizing and Overcoming Childhood Trauma

If Catherine can embark on a journey of healing, so can you. Here are signs and feelings to look out for, and advice on how to navigate the path to recovery:

Signs of Childhood Trauma:

1. **Persistent Negative Self-Image:**

   - Feeling unworthy, unattractive, or inherently flawed.

   - Internalizing negative beliefs about intelligence and capabilities.

2. **Difficulty Forming Relationships:**

   - Struggling to trust others or establish meaningful connections.

   - Fear of rejection and isolation.

3. **Low Self-Esteem and Self-Worth:**

   - Constant self-doubt and feelings of inadequacy.

   - Reluctance to pursue goals due to a belief in inevitable failure.

4. **Emotional Dysregulation:**

   - Difficulty managing emotions, leading to frequent mood swings.

   - Overwhelming feelings of sadness, anger, or anxiety.

5. **Avoidance of Triggers:**

   - Actively avoiding situations or people reminiscent of past trauma.

   - Developing coping mechanisms such as isolation or substance use.

Isolation in Plain Sight

Catherine's pleas for understanding echoed in the silent corridors of her own home. The community's collective judgment seeped through the walls, intensifying the isolation she felt. The more she cried out, the more she became a spectacle—a child deemed too sensitive for a world that failed to grasp the depth of her pain.

Catherine's isolation was a fortress, erected in plain sight. On the surface, she navigated the hallways of her school with a quiet grace, exchanging smiles and pleasantries as if she were part of the bustling tapestry of childhood camaraderie. Yet, her eyes betrayed a different story – a silent plea veiled behind a curtain of resilience.

In the cafeteria, Catherine occupied a corner table, surrounded by the chatter of her peers, yet untouched by their laughter. The lunchbox by her side held not just sandwiches but also the weight of her unspoken struggles. Her isolation wasn't a lack of company but a realm of emotional distance, a space where her pain echoed louder than the collective voices of her classmates.

At home, the isolation deepened. Behind the closed door of her room, Catherine found solace in the company of her thoughts, a refuge from the storm brewing in the living room. The laughter of sitcoms and the glow of the television provided a façade of familial normalcy, but Catherine remained a silent observer, a ghost within her own home.

The world outside remained oblivious to the isolation she wove into the fabric of her existence. Friends saw a girl who preferred solitude, teachers noticed a quiet student, and family perceived a child lost in daydreams. Yet, Catherine's isolation wasn't a choice; it was a fortress constructed brick by emotional brick to shield herself from the storms raging within.

Mrs. Anderson, became the first to breach the walls. Through subtle gestures and genuine interest, she invited Catherine into a space where isolation transformed into connection. It was in the sanctuary of trust that Catherine began to dismantle the barriers, sharing fragments of her hidden pain, and finding that vulnerability could be a bridge to understanding.

If only she could express her feelings and use the tools when she was home, her only thoughts when she walked home..

Unseen Pain

Behind closed doors, Catherine wrestled with emotions that felt like a tempest within. The community's dismissal of her feelings became a weight she carried, further fueling the belief that her struggles were inconsequential. In the shadows, she cried silent tears that mirrored the storm that raged in her heart.

Catherine's unseen pain was a silent symphony of sorrow, a melody that played in the quiet recesses of her heart, unnoticed by those who brushed past her in the hallways of life. In the gentle curve of her smile, in the flicker of her gaze, lay the unspoken chapters of a story that echoed with the weight of untold burdens.

Her unseen pain wore many disguises. In the classroom, she was a diligent student, her hand raised when prompted, her answers articulate and precise. Yet, behind the facade of academic prowess hid the struggle to concentrate, the battle against intrusive thoughts that threatened to overshadow the lesson at hand. The unseen pain manifested in the furrow of her brow, a subtle indication that the battlefield was not confined to textbooks.

At home, her unseen pain was a shadow cast over family dinners . The unspoken tension in the air, the hushed arguments that reverberated through closed doors about her, were the script of a drama Catherine never chose to audition for. Her pain lay in the gaps between spoken words, in the unshed tears that clung to her lashes like unspoken prayers for peace.

The playground became another stage for her unseen pain. As other children revealed in the joy of play, Catherine's pain found refuge in the sidelines, watching the world whirl around her while she stood in the eye of a storm that only she could feel. Unseen, unheard, and yet profoundly felt.

Mrs. Anderson, with her compassionate gaze, became the first to catch a glimpse of Catherine's unseen pain. Through art and storytelling, the young girl began to sketch the contours of her suffering, coloring outside the lines to express the chaos within. The canvas became a mirror reflecting the internal storms, and through the therapeutic strokes of a paintbrush, Catherine found a voice for her unseen pain and now had well over 60 paintings hidden from her family.

Looks and Beauty Standards

From a young age, Catherine was subjected to hurtful comments about her physical appearance. Her family, driven by societal beauty standards, criticized her features, labeling her as "ugly" and reinforcing harmful beauty norms. This constant barrage of negativity fueled a distorted self-image, leading Catherine to internalize these criticisms and question her own attractiveness. As Catherine navigated the storm within, the echoes of hurtful words cast a shadow on the reflection staring back at her. Self-hate, like an insidious vine, began to weave through the features she once embraced. Her full eyes, once a mirror to her vibrant spirit, became a source of internalized criticism. The curve of her lips, once expressive of joy, now carried the weight of judgments ingrained during her upbringing. In the journey to heal, Catherine grappled not only with the external traumas but with the internalized self-hate that threatened to obscure the beauty she failed to see in herself. Catherine raged, the discomfort with her own reflection manifested in a subtle yet profound change – her smile, once a beacon of genuine joy, gradually faded. The weight of self-doubt and internalized criticisms eroded the ease with which she once embraced happiness. Now, the act of smiling felt like navigating a minefield of insecurities. The genuine expressions of joy transformed into guarded gestures, revealing the silent struggle to reclaim a sense of comfort with herself.

In the wake of the storm within, Catherine's self-perception weathered a profound transformation. The belief in her own beauty, once a steadfast foundation, crumbled beneath the weight of past criticisms.

Compliments from strangers, once a source of validation, now stirred skepticism. Each kind word became tinged with suspicion, as she couldn't fathom the possibility that someone might see beauty where she had been taught to see flaws. The erosion of self-belief left her questioning the authenticity of praise, a casualty of the lingering shadows of childhood trauma. Colorism and Skin Tone Bias was yet another issue for her.

The Caribbean, like many regions, grapples with colorism, and Catherine became a victim of this insidious bias. Her family, perhaps influenced by deeply ingrained prejudices, perpetuated harmful notions that being too dark-skinned was a flaw. These remarks, rooted in colorist attitudes, left Catherine grappling with a sense of inferiority based on her skin tone.

The Weight of Labels

The "crazy child" label, once spoken in hushed tones, became an indelible mark on Catherine's identity. It followed her like a shadow, shaping the way others perceived her and influencing the opportunities she was afforded. The community's judgment seeped into the very fabric of her self-esteem.

The weight of labels draped over Catherine like an invisible cape, influencing not only how the world perceived her but also shaping her own sense of identity. In the crowded hallways of high school, where cliques and stereotypes held sway, Catherine found herself carrying the silent burden of expectations that came with the labels attached to her.

The label of "crazy, mad" trailed behind her, a tag earned through her love for literature, science, and an insatiable curiosity about the world. While her passion fueled her intellectual pursuits, the label confined her within the narrow expectations of societal norms. The weight of being a "crazy, mad, stupid" meant she was often expected to excel academically, but this expectation sometimes overshadowed her other talents and interests.

Simultaneously, Catherine grappled with the label of "quiet" – a descriptor often misunderstood as a lack of confidence or disinterest. The weight of this label cast a veil over the richness of her inner world, rendering her contributions and insights nearly invisible amid the cacophony of louder voices. The assumptions tied to her quiet demeanor became a heavy mantle, one that made it challenging for her authentic self to shine through.

The weight of labels extended into her personal life, where Catherine felt the constraints of being labeled "different" due to her unique interests and introverted nature. Society's tendency to categorize individuals created an invisible but palpable pressure to conform, to shed the labels that marked her as an outlier.

However, Catherine was determined to redefine the narrative. In the supportive environment fostered by Mrs. Anderson and a few genuine friends, she began to unravel the weight of labels. Through introspection and self-acceptance, Catherine discovered that these labels were not absolute truths but mere reflections of societal expectations.

The journey to shed the weight of labels became a transformative process for Catherine. It was about breaking free from stereotypes and celebrating the beauty of her individuality. The narrative shifted from the constraints of societal expectations to the empowerment found in embracing her authentic self.

As Catherine ventured further on her path of self-discovery, the weight of labels gradually lifted. The story became a testament to the resilience required to navigate the complexities of identity in a world quick to categorize. Catherine's journey was not about conforming to labels but about finding strength in authenticity, ultimately turning the weight of labels into wings that allowed her to soar beyond societal constraints.

Seeking Validation

Desperate for validation, Catherine yearned for someone to recognize the validity of her emotions. Yet, her cries for understanding fell on deaf ears. The community's collective dismissal ingrained a sense of worthlessness, as if her feelings were an inconvenience rather than a call for empathy.

Seeking validation became an unwitting companion on Catherine's journey, a constant yearning woven into the fabric of her daily existence. The weight of labels and the unseen struggles of childhood trauma had left her hungering for external affirmation, a reassurance that she was worthy, seen, and understood.

In the hallways of school, Catherine found herself casting furtive glances toward her peers, searching for nods of approval or smiles that could momentarily alleviate the ache within. The need for validation became a silent plea in her interactions, a desire to be acknowledged not just for her achievements but for the resilient spirit that thrived beneath the surface.

In classrooms, Catherine excelled academically, yet each high grade sought not just mastery of the subject but the approval of teachers and classmates alike. The thirst for validation transformed her pursuit of knowledge into a quest for external acknowledgment, a craving that echoed louder than the sound of the waves in the sea that followed her achievements.

At home, the dinner table became a stage where Catherine sought approval through every shared story and accomplishments, often shut down by name calling. The unspoken hope lingered in the air that, amidst the daily routine, her family would notice the effort, the silent battles waged, and validate the strength it took to navigate the complexities of her inner world.

The echoes of her unseen pain became quieter in the presence of Mrs. Anderson, her compassionate teacher. The validation found in Mrs. Anderson's encouragement became a lifeline, slowly reshaping Catherine's perception of herself. The realization that her worth transcended grades or societal expectations became a seed planted in fertile soil, sprouting the beginnings of self-validation.

However, the journey to self-validation was not linear. The shadows of labels and the scars of childhood trauma still lingered, occasionally casting doubt on Catherine's journey. Yet, in the quiet moments of introspection, she discovered that true validation came from within – a reservoir of strength, resilience, and authenticity that didn't require external approval.

Catherine's narrative of seeking validation became a story of self-discovery, of learning to appreciate her worth beyond societal metrics, and of understanding that the most profound validation came from embracing her authentic self. The journey continued, not to escape the need for validation, but to transform it into a compass guiding her towards a deeper, truer understanding of who she was and the value she carried within.

Longing for Connection

In her heart, Catherine carried a deep yearning for connection, for someone to see beyond the labels and acknowledge the pain she had long buried. Catherine's mother, unknowingly entrenched in the patterns of their past, used trigger words without realizing their impact. Her attempts to motivate often mirrored the hurtful language of Catherine's upbringing. The unintentional harm created a rift, leaving both mother and daughter stranded in a sea of miscommunication.

The community's misunderstanding left her grappling with an unspoken loneliness, a yearning for a sense of belonging that always seemed just out of reach.

Catherine's longing for connection flowed through the corridors of her heart, a soft melody that resonated with the yearning for genuine human bonds. Despite the bustling hallways of high school and the constant chatter of her peers, Catherine felt a profound sense of isolation – a solitude that only deepened her desire for authentic connection.

In the sea of faces that filled the classrooms, Catherine sought eyes that would meet hers with understanding, hearts that would resonate with the silent struggles she carried. Her yearning was not just for casual friendships but for connections that went beyond the surface, where words became a bridge to shared vulnerabilities and understanding.

The lunchroom, once a place of laughter and chatter, became a space where Catherine longed for a seat at a table where she could be seen and heard. The ache for connection manifested in stolen glances toward groups of friends, each laugh and shared moment a reminder of the connection she sought.

At home, she wished she could continue to paint or even show her family. Catherine yearned for a connection that went beyond the superficial exchanges. The dinner table became a silent battleground where unspoken conversations and dismissive action of her lingered in the air, and Catherine's longing for familial understanding became a poignant storm in her daily life.

Yet, the journey to connect was fraught with the shadows of labels and the scars of past pain. The fear of vulnerability sometimes eclipsed the longing, creating hesitations and doubts. Catherine grappled with the paradox of seeking connection while safeguarding the walls she had built to protect herself.

So she started to draw on the walls on the side of her bed.

As Catherine navigated the complexities of her longing, she discovered that connection wasn't solely dependent on external validation or familial understanding. True connection, she realized, began with an authentic connection to herself. The process of self-discovery became a crucial chapter in her narrative, fostering a profound connection with her own identity and allowing her to approach connections with others from a place of authenticity.

It was coming along to the holidays and Catherine's family was making revelations to accommodate families that would be flying in from Canada and the Uk.

One day, as sunlight danced through the window, Catherine's long-hidden sanctuary of creativity was accidentally uncovered by her older cousin Alex.

He had traveled earlier to help with the home renovation as he had a construction company in Canada. In the quiet corners of their cramped home, he stumbled upon a treasure of over 400 paintings that had been carefully concealed, each canvas a testament to Catherine's silent resilience. Amazed by the artwork he questioned who had made them. No one had an answer, everyone was clueless.

The vibrant strokes on the canvases whispered stories of unspoken pain, whispered prayers for healing, and bursts of color that defied the darkness that once shrouded her. As her siblings looked marveled at the emotions laid bare in the strokes and hues, they realized that Catherine's art was not just a collection of paintings but a powerful expression of the strength she carried within. The discovery became a bridge as people in the community started to gather around , connecting them to the depths of her soul and sparking conversations that began to dissolve the silence surrounding the storm that had shaped her world each painting labeled HealingExpressions. Catherin could see the large crowd from the hill top and became concerned that something had happened to her family. She dropped her school bag an ran as fast as she could.

Yet, despite the storm within, Catherine clung to a flicker of resilience. A whisper of hope that someday, someone would see beyond the facade, recognize the strength that lay beneath the scars, and offer a lifeline to pull her from the depths of the tempest she navigated alone. The story of Catherine, etched in the sands of the Caribbean, remained a poignant reminder of the unseen battles fought within the hearts of those who carry the weight of childhood trauma.

Catherine's family, unfortunately, became the architects of the emotional tempest that swirled within her. The wounds inflicted by their words cut deep, leaving lasting scars on her self-esteem and sense of worth.

Her Intellectual Devaluation The denigration extended beyond physical appearance to Catherine's intellectual capabilities. She was repeatedly told she would never amount to anything, creating a pervasive belief that she was inherently incapable. This undermined her confidence in academic pursuits and set the stage for a constant internal struggle to prove her worth in Comparison with Siblings:

Catherine's family dynamic further exacerbated her emotional turmoil. Constant comparisons with her siblings, whether in looks or achievements, created an environment of competition rather than support. Each accomplishment by her siblings felt like a spotlight on her perceived shortcomings, intensifying the storm of inadequacy within her.Impact on Self-Esteem

The cumulative effect of these put-downs took a toll on Catherine's self-esteem. She internalized the belief that she was inherently flawed, both in appearance and intellect. This damaged self-perception permeated every aspect of her life, hindering her ability to form healthy relationships and pursue her goals with confidence.

Cycle of Emotional Abuse The emotional abuse Catherine endured formed a toxic cycle, perpetuating itself through generations. The damaging words she heard mirrored the messages her family had likely internalized themselves. Breaking free from this cycle required not only personal resilience but also a conscious effort to challenge and reject the harmful narratives that had become ingrained.

The Journey to Healing

As Catherine matured, she began to recognize the impact of the community's perception on her mental well-being. With resilience as her guide, she sought therapy, slowly untangling the knots of judgment and working towards reclaiming her narrative.

In this Caribbean tale, Catherine's experience underscores the profound effects of community judgment on an individual's mental health. It serves as a reminder that, beneath the surface, every "crazy child" may be navigating a storm that only empathy and understanding can calm.

Sensory Waves

As she was running the aroma of spices wafted through the air, Catherine couldn't escape the memories of her family's cutting words and how the kitchen, once a place of warmth, became a battleground of emotional turmoil. The clinking of utensils echoed the harshness of her family's criticisms. Out of breath she stopped mid way thinking what if they think i did something to harm them a wave of mixed emotions got the best of her.

Catherine could make out a few people out of the crowd, With her heart being fast and now jogging slowly. She could hear someone say " she har deh ,Catherine come quick' the voice was familiar one of a shopkeeper Mrs Ruby her voice was deep on strong for a lady. Ruby's voice went through her body touching her bone as she thought something was extremely wrong. not sure if she should turn back and run the other way, while the crowd turned to see her she could see a few of her paintings being held up by her 3 young sisters.

As she got closer Catherine remembered conversations with her family, trigger words lurked beneath the surface. Each mention of her appearance or intelligence sent shockwaves through her emotions. The phrases once casually thrown around in her household were now like verbal landmines, waiting to detonate her fragile sense of self-worth. This is know as Verbal Landmines.

As Catherine's cousin, Alex, unveiled each canvas, Alex's eyes widened in awe, and a warm applause echoed through the crowd. Catherine, once accustomed to the shadows, stood in the spotlight of appreciation, her heart swelling with a mix of vulnerability and pride.

For the first time, her paintings, born from the depths of pain, were transforming into a source of joy for others. As the applause reverberated, Catherine felt an unexpected surge of happiness. The colors that had once reflected her internal storms now radiated a different energy—one that resonated with the hearts of those who witnessed her art. In that moment, Catherine realized the transformative power of turning pain into something beautiful, and she took solace in the profound connection her art forged between her own healing journey and the joy it brought to others.

As Catherine's cousin, Alex, marveled at her incredible talent, he couldn't help but express his amazement. With a gentle smile, he asked her siblings and parents how they had never known about her remarkable artistic skills. Her family, taken aback by the revelation, admitted they had been oblivious to the beautiful world she had crafted within the strokes of her paintings.

Intrigued by the potential he saw, Alex shared that he had connections with a prominent art gallery in Canada specializing in unique pieces like Catherine's. His business associates, whom he had met during college, were passionate about promoting transformative art. He speculated on the worth of her paintings, not just in monetary value but in the potential to showcase them to a broader audience.

As the realization dawned on Catherine's family, a mix of surprise and pride filled the room. The narrative of Catherine's art, once confined to the shadows, was now unfolding under the spotlight of opportunity. The question lingered in the air—how had they missed this extraordinary talent? The journey of unveiling not only Catherine's art but also the layers of her resilience had just begun.

Alex felt compelled to understand the stories woven into each masterpiece. With a gentle curiosity, he asked her to share the narratives behind the art that had been concealed for so long. Catherine, drawing a breath, began to unveil the emotions encapsulated in her brushstrokes.

She pointed to a poignant piece where a crown adorned the heads of figures with shadowed faces. With a calm but resolute voice, she explained how each person represented in the painting had played a role in the storm that once consumed her. The crown, a symbol of the power they once held over her, now stood as a visual testament to her reclamation of strength.

As she described each stroke, Catherine transformed the pain into a language of healing. The hues and contours of her art became a narrative of resilience, speaking volumes about the battles she fought within herself. Her cousin, captivated by the raw authenticity of her stories, listened with an understanding that transcended words.

In that shared moment, the paintings became more than mere art—they became a map of Catherine's journey, guiding her through the tumultuous waters of her past. As each canvas unveiled its secrets, a sense of catharsis filled the room, and the weight of unspoken pain began to lift.

Alex, moved by the profound stories embedded in Catherine's paintings, felt a mix of empathy and admiration for her strength. Witnessing her bare her soul through art, he recognized the gravity of the healing journey she had undertaken. Motivated by a deep desire to support her, Alex took intentional steps to make her feel seen and valued.

Firstly, he expressed genuine appreciation for her artistry, highlighting the emotional depth and resilience evident in every stroke. Alex acknowledged the courage it took for Catherine to share such intimate narratives, creating a safe space where vulnerability was met with understanding.

Sensitive to the impact of her past, Alex offered words of affirmation, emphasizing the strength he saw in her ability to transform pain into something beautiful. He reassured her that the worth of her art extended beyond any monetary value—it was a testament to her triumph over adversity.

Understanding the potential of her paintings, Alex took initiative in connecting her with his associates at the Canadian art gallery. He believed that showcasing her work to a wider audience could not only provide a platform for her talent but also contribute to the broader conversation on healing through art.

In the days that followed, Alex remained a pillar of support, actively participating in discussions about Catherine's art and ensuring that her family fully appreciated the significance of her talent. Through his actions and words, he became a catalyst for bolstering Catherine's sense of worth and validation.

By fostering an environment of understanding, encouragement, and opportunity, Alex played a pivotal role in helping Catherine reclaim her narrative and find solace in the transformative power of her own art.

Alex's connections with the Canadian art gallery bore unexpected fruit as potential buyers expressed profound interest in Catherine's evocative paintings. In a gesture that reflected not just a monetary valuation but a deep appreciation for the narratives she had poured onto canvas, they offered a staggering sixty thousand dollars for a collection of 42 of her artworks.

The offer, accompanied by genuine admiration for Catherine's talent, extended beyond financial compensation. These buyers recognized the transformative nature of her art and saw an opportunity to amplify her impact on a grander scale. In a heartening twist, they proposed displaying the remaining pieces in their prestigious art gallery, where they would be part of an upcoming auction.

The prospect of her paintings reaching an international audience and finding homes in the hearts of art enthusiasts brought a mix of excitement and awe. The opportunity to contribute to the broader conversation on healing through art resonated deeply with Catherine, and the recognition of her work's value was a validation that surpassed her wildest dreams.

As the wheels were set in motion for this unexpected chapter, Catherine faced a crossroads of possibilities. The journey that began in the quiet corners of her home had taken an unforeseen turn, transforming her art from a deeply personal expression to a beacon of inspiration for others. The auction, looming on the horizon, held the promise of not only showcasing her talent but also spreading ripples of healing and empowerment far beyond the shores of her past.

Eager to share her newfound success with someone who had played a significant role in her journey, Catherine invited Alex to meet her teacher, Mrs. Anderson. As they gathered, a sense of gratitude and excitement filled the room. Mrs. Anderson, a beacon of support throughout Catherine's educational years, observed the vibrant transformation .

Alex extended the opportunity to Mrs. Anderson, recognizing her pivotal role in fostering Catherine's resilience. Holding one of Catherine's paintings, Alex conveyed the potential for her art to reach new heights in Canada. With a warmth that transcended borders, he suggested the prospect of Mrs. Anderson accompanying them on this unexpected journey, emphasizing the positive impact her guidance could continue to have.

Mrs. Anderson, touched by the gesture and proud of Catherine's growth, welcomed the idea. She saw in Catherine's paintings not just artistic brilliance but a testimony to the strength that had blossomed under her care. Encouraging Catherine to paint through her pain had not only cultivated artistic expression but had become a means of therapeutic healing.

As the trio contemplated the possibilities that lay ahead, the connection between teacher, student, and family forged a bridge of shared accomplishments. The journey that began with the storm within was evolving into a narrative of resilience, support, and the transformative power of art. The prospect of flying back to Canada with not just paintings but with a teacher who had been an unwavering anchor promised to make this journey even more profound.

Therapeutic Tides

While in Canada, Catherine immersed herself in therapeutic tides, navigating the waves of healing that embraced her newfound environment. The support and opportunities that unfolded became the backdrop against which she continued her journey of overcoming childhood trauma.

Professional Guidance:

Catherine sought the expertise of a therapist experienced in trauma recovery. The therapeutic sessions provided a structured space for her to explore the layers of her past and develop coping mechanisms for the present.

Art as Therapy:

Continuing the practice Mrs. Anderson encouraged, Catherine painted through her pain. The Canadian art scene became a canvas for her emotional expressions, each stroke a testament to her resilience and newfound sense of self.

Community Support:

Surrounded by a community that valued her art and appreciated the stories it told, Catherine found solace in connection. The understanding and empathy she received fueled her sense of belonging, countering the isolation she once felt.

Self-Discovery Through Education:

Catherine engaged in educational pursuits that were driven by personal growth rather than external validation. The joy of learning became a source of empowerment, helping her redefine her relationship with education.

As the therapeutic tides washed over her, Catherine witnessed the gradual transformation of her internal landscape. The steps she took, guided by resilience and a newfound sense of agency, became beacons of hope for those on similar paths of healing. In Canada, surrounded by supportive allies and therapeutic opportunities, Catherine continued to reclaim her narrative and rewrite the story of her own resilience.

Empowerment Narratives

In Canada, Catherine crafted a tapestry of a better life, weaving together threads of resilience, art, and newfound opportunities. Surrounded by a supportive community, she embarked on a journey of personal growth and empowerment.

Catherine's passion for art not only flourished but also became a cornerstone of her new life. Her paintings found homes in galleries, telling stories of triumph and resilience. The therapeutic tides of Canada provided a nurturing environment for her to heal, and each stroke of her brush became a celebration of her strength.

Amidst her personal successes, Catherine extended an open invitation to her beloved teacher, Mrs. Anderson, welcoming her to spend holidays and share in the joy of her newfound life. The bonds forged in the classroom transformed into enduring connections that spanned continents.

Catherine, driven by a profound sense of responsibility, also made it a point to influence change in her old school back in the Caribbean. Recognizing the importance of addressing childhood trauma, she implemented initiatives within after-school programs to create spaces where students could openly discuss and process their experiences. This commitment to fostering understanding and empathy became a legacy, leaving an indelible mark on the community she once called home.

As Catherine continued to thrive in her Canadian haven, her story became an inspiration—a testament to the transformative power of resilience and the unwavering spirit that emerges from the storm within. Her better life not only illuminated her personal triumphs but also became a beacon of hope for others navigating the turbulent seas of their own pasts.

In the midst of the turbulent storm within her, Catherine found the strength to take steps toward healing and resilience. Recognizing the need to confront her childhood trauma, she embarked on a journey of self-discovery and recovery. Here are a few of the steps she took

1. **Therapeutic Exploration:**

Catherine sought the guidance of a compassionate therapist who provided a safe space for her to unpack the emotional baggage she carried. Through therapy, she explored the roots of her insecurities, addressing the wounds inflicted during her upbringing.

2. **Self-Reflection and Acceptance:**

Confronting the distorted self-image ingrained by years of hurtful words, Catherine engaged in deep self-reflection. She learned to challenge and reframe the negative narratives, gradually accepting and embracing her true identity, beyond the judgments imposed upon her.

3. **Support Networks:**

Building a network of understanding and empathetic friends became a crucial pillar in Catherine's recovery. Connecting with individuals who acknowledged her struggles and offered genuine support provided a sense of belonging and shattered the isolation that had defined much of her life.

4. **Educational Empowerment:**

Catherine rekindled her academic pursuits, not as a pursuit of external validation but as a means of personal empowerment. She rediscovered the joy of learning, dismantling the limiting beliefs that had hindered her educational journey.

5. **Mindfulness and Self-Care:**

Incorporating mindfulness practices and prioritizing self-care became integral to Catherine's healing process. Whether through meditation, journaling, or engaging in activities that brought her joy, she learned to nurture her mental and emotional well-being.

6. **Setting Boundaries:**

Catherine recognized the importance of setting boundaries with her family, creating a protective space where she could heal without being engulfed by the toxic patterns of the past. This empowered her to define her own identity independently of the expectations imposed on her.

7. **Advocacy and Empowerment:**

As she progressed on her journey, Catherine became an advocate for mental health awareness. Sharing her story empowered others to break the silence surrounding childhood trauma, fostering a community of support and understanding.

8. **Cultural Reclamation:**

Embracing her Caribbean roots became a source of strength for Catherine. She rediscovered pride in her heritage, celebrating the richness of her culture and challenging the narrow standards that had once dictated her worth.

Through these transformative steps, Catherine not only weathered the storm within but emerged as a resilient force, reshaping her narrative and inspiring others on their own paths to healing. The scars remained, but they became symbols of triumph rather than reminders of defeat.

Catherine's relationship with her mother, once a source of comfort and support, deteriorated into a challenging and strained dynamic due to the toxic patterns that unfolded during her upbringing. The journey to repair their relationship involved both parties taking intentional steps to heal and rebuild trust.

Just a few things to look out for

1. **Hurtful Remarks:**

Catherine's mother, influenced by societal beauty standards and perhaps her own insecurities, contributed to the negative comments about Catherine's looks and skin tone. The hurtful remarks, intended or not, created a rift between mother and daughter.

2. **Expectations and Comparison:**

The constant comparisons between Catherine and her siblings, fueled by unrealistic expectations, strained the mother-daughter bond. Catherine felt overshadowed and unappreciated, while her mother unknowingly perpetuated a harmful cycle of emotional abuse.

3. **Lack of Emotional Support:**

Catherine yearned for emotional support and affirmation from her mother, but the unaddressed trauma prevented the mother from recognizing the depth of Catherine's struggles. The absence of a nurturing environment contributed to the emotional distance between them.

Steps to Overcome

1. **Open Communication:**

Both Catherine and her mother took the courageous step of engaging in open and honest communication. They created a space where feelings could be expressed without judgment, allowing for a deeper understanding of each other's perspectives.

2. **Therapeutic Intervention:**

Recognizing the need for professional help, they decided to attend family therapy together. A skilled therapist guided them through the process of acknowledging past hurts, fostering empathy, and developing healthier communication patterns.

3. **Acknowledgment and Apology:**

Catherine's mother acknowledged the impact of her words and actions on her daughter. A sincere apology became a crucial step in rebuilding trust, as it conveyed a willingness to take responsibility for the pain caused.

4. **Education on Mental Health:**

Both sought education on the effects of childhood trauma and its long-term impact on mental health. Understanding the psychological consequences helped them empathize with each other's experiences and fostered a sense of shared responsibility for healing.

5. **Setting Boundaries:**

Together, they established clear and healthy boundaries to ensure a more respectful and supportive environment. This involved addressing patterns of criticism and comparison, allowing Catherine the space to develop her identity without the weight of unrealistic expectations.

6. **Counseling for Individual Growth:**

In addition to family therapy, Catherine and her mother engaged in individual counseling to address their own personal challenges. This allowed them to work on personal growth, self-awareness, and emotional well-being.

7. **Quality Time and Rebuilding Trust:**

They consciously spent quality time together, engaging in activities that fostered positive interactions. Rebuilding trust required consistent efforts to create new, positive memories that replaced the negative associations from the past.

8. **Cultural Understanding:**

Understanding and appreciating each other's perspectives within the context of their Caribbean heritage became an important aspect of their reconciliation. Embracing cultural differences fostered a deeper connection and a shared sense of identity.

Through these collective efforts, Catherine and her mother gradually moved from a place of discord to a more harmonious relationship. The healing journey was ongoing, but the commitment to understanding, empathy, and growth laid the foundation for a healthier bond between mother and daughter.

Advice for Healing:

1. **Seek Professional Support:**

   - Reach out to a therapist or counselor experienced in trauma. Professional guidance provides a structured and supportive environment for healing.

2. **Open Communication:**

   - Share your feelings with trusted friends, family, or a support group. Open communication is a crucial step in breaking the silence surrounding trauma.

3. **Educate Yourself:**

   - Learn about the impact of childhood trauma on mental health. Understanding the root causes helps in addressing and processing the emotional wounds.

4. **Practice Self-Compassion:**

   - Be kind to yourself. Challenge negative self-talk and replace it with affirming statements. Self-compassion is a vital aspect of the healing journey.

5. **Set Boundaries:**

   - Establish healthy boundaries with individuals who contribute to negative patterns. This may involve limiting contact or clearly communicating expectations for respectful interactions.

6. **Engage in Self-Care:**

   - Prioritize self-care activities that promote mental and emotional well-being. This includes activities that bring joy, relaxation, and a sense of balance.

7. **Build Support Networks:**

   - Surround yourself with understanding and empathetic individuals. Seek out friends, family, or support groups where you can share experiences and receive encouragement.

8. **Cultural Reclamation:**

   - Embrace and celebrate your cultural identity. Reconnecting with your roots can be a powerful source of strength and pride.

9. **Educational Pursuits:**

   - Rediscover the joy of learning for personal growth rather than external validation. Pursue educational goals at your own pace and in areas that bring fulfillment.

10. **Mindfulness Practices:**

    - Incorporate mindfulness and meditation into your routine to stay present and reduce anxiety. Mindfulness techniques help break the cycle of rumination on past traumas.

Remember, healing is a unique journey, and progress may be gradual. You deserve support and understanding as you navigate the path toward recovery. If Catherine can overcome her childhood trauma, you can too.

Without the crucial intervention and support that Catherine eventually sought, the trajectory of her life would have taken a darker turn, overshadowed by the unaddressed wounds of her childhood. As the years passed, the storm within Catherine would have intensified. The weight of unresolved trauma could have led to

Isolation and Despair:

Catherine, unable to break free from the chains of her past, withdrew further into isolation. The persistent negative self-image and feelings of unworthiness gnawed at her spirit, leaving her stranded in a sea of despair.

Strained Relationships:

The toxic patterns of her childhood permeated her adult relationships. Intimacy became a battleground, as Catherine struggled to trust and connect with others. The fear of rejection, deeply rooted in the traumas of her upbringing, sabotaged any potential for meaningful connections.

Stunted Personal Growth:

Academic and personal pursuits that once held promise became distant dreams. The belief that she was inherently incapable echoed louder than any encouragement from the outside world. Catherine's potential remained untapped, buried beneath layers of self-doubt.

Emotional Turmoil:

The emotional dysregulation intensified, with mood swings becoming more unpredictable. The unresolved trauma manifested in bouts of overwhelming sadness, anger, and anxiety, each episode pushing her further into the abyss of mental and emotional turmoil.

Repeating Patterns:

Tragically, the cycle of abuse and trauma might have extended to future generations. Catherine, never having confronted and healed from her own past, may have inadvertently perpetuated harmful patterns in her own relationships and family dynamics.

Lost Opportunities for Healing:

Without the therapeutic intervention and the support she eventually sought, Catherine missed opportunities for healing and personal growth. The vibrant colors of life remained muted, and the potential for a fulfilling, empowered existence slipped through her fingers.

A Life Unfulfilled:

Ultimately, the storm within Catherine would have continued to dictate the narrative of her life, leaving her trapped in a cycle of pain and despair. The vibrant, resilient spirit she once possessed would have withered, leaving behind the echoes of what could have been.

It is a stark reminder that the impact of untreated childhood trauma can reverberate throughout a person's life, affecting not only their well-being but the trajectory of their entire existence. Seeking help and breaking the silence surrounding such trauma is a crucial step towards reclaiming one's life and authoring a different, more hopeful narrative.

The calm after the storm

The importance of addressing childhood trauma cannot be overstated, as it can significantly impact one's mental and emotional well-being throughout life. Recognizing the signs and dealing with it promptly are crucial steps toward breaking the cycle of generational pain. Catherine's journey serves as a testament to the transformative power of facing and healing from childhood trauma.

As an amazing and impactful woman, Catherine not only reclaimed herself but also strengthened family relationships that had once been strained by the echoes of the past. Her resilience and commitment to healing became a source of inspiration, illustrating that the scars of childhood trauma do not define one's destiny.

Catherine, now a beacon of empowerment, took it upon herself to advocate for awareness within her community. By openly sharing her story and providing advice, she became a catalyst for change. Her message was clear: childhood trauma should not be shoved under the rug. Instead, it should be acknowledged, discussed, and met with empathy and support.

In her advocacy, Catherine highlighted the importance of recognizing signs of childhood trauma, such as triggers and trigger words, and the significance of seeking professional help. By fostering an environment that encourages open conversations about mental health, Catherine aimed to break down the stigma surrounding trauma and create a community where healing is prioritized.

Through her own experiences, Catherine became a guiding light for others, proving that the journey to reclaim oneself is not only possible but transformative. Her impact rippled through her family, community, and beyond, leaving an indelible mark on the collective understanding of the importance of addressing and healing from childhood trauma.

In addition to her advocacy, Catherine has extended her impact by opening an art gallery dedicated to youth and young adults. This space serves not only as a showcase for their artistic expressions but also as a haven for healing. The gallery hosts a free after-school program, providing a creative outlet for young minds to explore the transformative power of art.

Understanding the financial challenges that many families face, Catherine has gone a step further. Recognizing the importance of mental health support, she has ensured that an on-site therapist is available. This therapist is committed to providing affordable services tailored to the needs of low-income families within the community.

Catherine's art gallery has become more than just a venue for artistic exploration; it's a sanctuary for healing, a place where the scars of childhood trauma are met with understanding, compassion, and the empowering brushstrokes of resilience. Through her philanthropic efforts, Catherine continues to be a beacon of change, reinforcing the notion that everyone deserves access to healing spaces and the support necessary for reclaiming their narratives.

www.ingramcontent.com/pod-product-compliance
Lightning Source LLC
Chambersburg PA
CBHW061516040426
42450CB00008B/1648